MAKING SPEECHES

Grade 5

By
Shirley C. Granahan

Published by Frank Schaffer Publications
an imprint of

Author: Shirley C. Granahan
Editors: Kathryn Wheeler, Cary Malaski

Children's Publishing

Published by Frank Schaffer
An imprint of McGraw-Hill Children's Publishing

Send all inquiries to:
McGraw-Hill Children's Publishing
3195 Wilson Drive NW
Grand Rapids, Michigan 49544

Making Speeches—grade 5
ISBN: 0-7424-1845-6

1 2 3 4 5 6 7 8 9 MAL 08 07 06 05 04 03

The McGraw·Hill Companies

Table of Contents

Note to the Teacher 4

Everyone Gives Speeches 5

Know the Reason 6

Know Your Audience 7

Choosing a Topic 8

Kinds of Speeches 9

A Speech to Demonstrate 10–11

A Speech to Inform 12–13

A Speech to Persuade.................14–15

A Speech to Entertain 16–17

Research 18

Making Notes and Cue Cards 19

Outlining...................................20–21

Grammar Check 22–23

The Speech: The Opening 24–25

The Speech: The Body 26–27

The Speech: The Conclusion 28–29

Read and Revise...............................30

Choosing and Using Visual Aids 31

Delivery: Your Voice 32

Delivery: Your Body Language 33

Practice and Check...........................34

Nerves: Good News or Bad? 35

Examine a Speech 36–37

Interview and Introduce 38–39

Accept an Award..............................40

Make a Public Announcement...........41

Give a Review..................................42

Be Entertaining................................43

Be Persuasive...................................44

Speak to a New Audience 45

Answer Key 46–47

Making Speeches Scoring Rubric 48

Note to the Teacher

As educators, we know that students need to practice their oral communication skills. But creating good speechwriters and speechmakers requires a step-by-step process in order to lay a foundation for this crucial skill. *Making Speeches* was designed to help teachers get students on track by combining writing and public speaking skills.

Making Speeches teaches students about the basic types of speeches and the step-by-step process for planning, writing, and delivering them. Students discover that how they look and sound when making a speech is just as important as how they write it. A well-written speech is worthless if no one is interested enough to listen! Activities in *Making Speeches* provide opportunities for students to critique speeches as well as to write and give speeches.

The exercises help students review the requirements of any writing process—proper punctuation, complete sentences, topic or main idea statements, and details to support the main idea. Students also explore the use of descriptive and persuasive words to capture the audience's attention, get the message across, and/or change the audience's point of view.

The speech-writing activities in *Making Speeches* permit young writers to generate their own ideas and practice working with those ideas. Variety of choice is encouraged. Standard exercises also help students strengthen comprehension and critical-thinking skills.

Time and patience are necessary in order to develop good speech-writing and speaking skills. Students need to build self-confidence in their ability to choose topics, put their ideas into words, and get those ideas across in presentations. Some students may have difficulty letting go of their need to read what they wrote rather than speaking naturally using a minimum of notes. *Making Speeches* can help students gain confidence as public speakers who know what they want to say and say it.

Name ______________________________ Date ______________________________

Everyone Gives Speeches

Everyone is a speechmaker. You talk and other people listen. That's giving a speech. When you explain to a friend how to kick a soccer ball, you're giving a speech. When you tell people about a movie, you're giving a speech.

Those are unrehearsed, or impromptu, speeches. This book focuses on planned, or rehearsed, speeches.

Before you can write a planned speech, you need to know:

- the occasion for the speech.
- who your audience will be.
- the topic of the speech.
- the kind of speech you want to give.

Read each speech excerpt below. Write **I** (for impromptu) if you think the excerpt was unrehearsed. Write **P** (for planned) if you think the excerpt was rehearsed.

1. _____ Last summer I was on my Grandpa's farm. It was getting dark and I was getting scared. I looked for my Grandpa and found him in the barn. Then this thing ZOOMed at me from the rafters! I screamed, but Grandpa laughed. He said bats wouldn't hurt me. After that, I only went to the barn during the day. That's when the bats sleep!

2. _____ Because they fly, bats are often mistaken for birds. But bats are mammals. Their young are born alive and get milk from their mothers. Bats can't walk or run because their feet aren't very strong. Bats' feet are just strong enough for the animals to hold on to a perch while they hang upside down, which is how they rest or sleep. To start flying, they just drop from their perches.

3. _____ There are about 900 known species of bats. They live in all but the coldest climates. The little brown bat is most common in North America. The animal is just 3 1/2 inches long and weighs about 1/2 ounce. It spends the day in caves, in hollow trees, in attics, and under roofs. During the winter, bats hibernate in caves.

4. _____ Did you know that vampire bats bite animals and sleeping humans and lap the blood that oozes out? I saw this movie last week. This guy slept in a coffin during the day. At night, he went looking for people to bite. Their blood kept him alive. Can you believe he was 300 years old?

Name ______________________________ Date ______________________________

Know the Reason

People give speeches for all kinds of reasons. Some speeches are made at official or formal events, such as an election speech on TV. Other speeches are made at casual events, such as a thank-you speech at a party.

Circle the best answer for each situation.

1. Someone would most likely give a formal speech to—
   A. tell voters to get out and vote.
   B. thank people for an award he or she won.
   C. encourage people to help clean up the environment.
   D. all of the above

2. Someone would most likely give a casual speech—
   A. in Congress.
   B. at a birthday party.
   C. at the opening of a new school.
   D. at a graduation ceremony.

Read each example below. Write **F** if the speech is for a formal occasion or **C** if the speech is for a casual occasion.

3. _____ Hi. Welcome to the reunion of the class of '85. I haven't seen some of you since we graduated. That was a long time ago! Now most of us are parents. And some of us have kids who attend this school. Can you believe some of the same teachers are still here?

4. _____ Thank you for that generous welcome. As you know, I've spent many years living with the animals of the African jungle. I have watched the populations of some species dwindle as the animals become threatened or endangered. Many species were overhunted and much of their habitat was cleared for building roads and villages. We all must help save our wildlife. And that's what I'm here to talk to you about tonight.

5. _____ This is a first for me! I've never won anything before! I'm really overwhelmed. I'd like to thank the record company for taking a chance on an unknown. I'd like to thank my manager and agents—and, of course, Mike, for writing the song for me. Without his genius, I wouldn't be standing here as Best New Artist!

Name ______________________________ Date ______________________________

Know Your Audience

You're going to give a speech. But to whom? You may speak to groups that are younger or older than you or to groups that are a mixture of both. Good speechmakers can speak to a variety of audiences on the same topic. They just adjust their topic to fit the group.

Circle the letter next to the audience for whom the speech was given.

1. Did you see a dinosaur on your way to school today? Of course not! That's because dinosaurs lived long, long ago. We can see models of them in museums. Some of the models even move, but they're not alive. Dinosaurs have been extinct, or no longer on Earth, for millions of years.

   A. a group of senior citizens

   B. a college science class

   C. a kindergarten class

   D. a group of science teachers

2. Since there were no cameras in prehistoric times, we have no old photos of dinosaurs. So early scientists used *if-then* thinking to decide what colors to put on museum models: "**If** dinosaurs were lizard like, **then** they probably looked a lot like today's lizards. And **if** today's lizards are gray, brown, or green, **then** dinosaurs were probably the same colors." That's why most of our dinosaur models have the same colors as today's lizards.

   A. visitors to a natural history museum

   B. a meeting of the math club

   C. a pep rally for the high school football team

   D. a class reunion dinner party

3. When telling young people about prehistoric animals, stress that prehistoric means "before written records." Remind the children that no one knows exactly why dinosaurs are extinct because no one was around to witness what happened. But scientists do have theories. Most of the theories relate to changes in Earth's climate after a gigantic meteorite crashed into Earth's surface. One interesting theory is that increasingly hot weather caused more male than female dinosaurs to develop. In other words, dinosaurs became extinct because there were no females to increase the population.

   A. a fifth-grade class

   B. visitors at a new mall

   C. science teachers

   D. a parent-teacher meeting

Name ______________________________ Date ______________________________

Choosing a Topic

Now you must choose a topic. Pick something that interests you and that you can make interesting for others. Be careful not to choose a topic that's too big to cover in a short speech.

Ask yourself the following questions:

- Does this topic interest me?
- Do I know enough about the topic, or can I find out enough about it?
- Can I make the topic interesting to the audience?
- Can I cover the topic in the time allotted for my speech?

Read the main-idea statements below, and write the topic of each statement on the line. This statement should tell you the most important point of the speech.

Topic	Main-Idea Statement
________________	During the Revolution, a teenage girl named Sybil Luddington rode all night to warn people that the British were coming.
________________	Lightning comes before thunder in a storm because a flash of electricity (lightning) heats the air, resulting in a loud crash (thunder).
________________	The history of computers began centuries ago with an ancient calculator called an abacus that was used to solve math problems by moving beads on rods or wires.

Now write a main-idea statement for each topic listed below.

Topic	Main-Idea Statement
1. Basketball	____
2. Magnets	____
3. Dinosaurs	____
4. Rap music	____
5. Pets	____

Name ______________________________ Date ______________________________

Kinds of Speeches

There are four basic types of speeches.

Speeches are given:

- **to demonstrate**—shows a step-by-step process.
- **to inform**—gives the audience information.
- **to persuade**—convinces the audience of something.
- **to entertain**—makes people laugh.

Once you've decided what to talk about, you should write your purpose in a statement form. Here are some examples.

- I'll demonstrate to the audience how to make a model ship.
- I'll inform the audience about downhill skiing.
- I'll persuade the audience to give money for the new children's library.
- I'll entertain the audience with details of the first time I baked a cake.

Sometimes a speech can inform and entertain. Or you might give a demonstration speech that also persuades your audience to try the activity. Below are four purposes Rebecca found for her speech about cross-country skiing.

- I'll demonstrate to the audience how to put on skis.
- I'll inform the audience about the difference between downhill and cross-country skiing.
- I'll persuade the audience to start a ski club at school.
- I'll entertain the audience with stories about why people change from downhill to cross-country skiing.

Now pick a topic you might use for each different kind of speech. Finish each sentence. You don't have to use these topics later, but you can.

1. I could demonstrate to an audience how to ______________________________.
2. I could inform an audience about ______________________________.
3. I could persuade an audience to ______________________________.
4. I could entertain an audience by ______________________________.

Name ______________________________ Date ______________________________

A Speech to Demonstrate

In this kind of speech, you show the audience how to do something. Think of something you do very well.

Below are some topics other fifth graders have used for demonstration speeches. Put stars by the four topics that interest you the most.

how to identify the constellations	how to make and write with invisible ink
how to repot flowers	how to make bread
how to play the drums	how to find percentages
how to clean a chocolate stain	how to make peanut butter fudge
how to build a fire	how to refinish an old table
how to organize a closet	how to find words in a dictionary
how to knit a sweater	how to do gymnastics
how to shovel snow safely	how to set a table
how to write in Japanese	how to fix a jammed printer
how to use a video camera	how to write a check

In a good demonstration speech, you give step-by-step directions for an activity. The directions must be clear and easy to understand. They must also be in the correct order.

Below are directions for making macaroni and cheese. Number them from 1–12 in the correct order.

1. Cooking Macaroni and Cheese

___ Cook the macaroni for 11 minutes.
___ Serve and enjoy!
___ Get a box of macaroni and cheese, a pot, a spoon, and a measuring cup.
___ Open the cheese packet.
___ Put three cups of water into the pot.
___ Add cheese to the hot macaroni.
___ Put the pot on the stove, and turn on the heat.
___ Drain the macaroni. Return to pot.
___ Boil the water.
___ Stir until the cheese melts.
___ Open the box and add the macaroni to the boiling water.
___ Turn off the heat.

Name ______________________ Date ______________________

A Speech to Demonstrate (cont.)

Read each set of step-by-step directions below. Write the topic of the demonstration speech on the line.

2. Topic: ______________________

1. Get four placemats from the drawer.
2. Put the placemats on top of the table, one on each side.
3. Get four plates and four glasses from the cabinet.
4. Put one plate and glass on each placemat.
5. Get four knives, four forks, and four spoons from the drawer.
6. Place a fork on the left side of each plate.
7. Place a knife on the right side of each plate.
8. Place a spoon on the right side of each knife.
9. Get four napkins from the cabinet.
10. Fold and place a napkin under each fork.

3. Topic: ______________________

1. Get a lemon, a small knife, a glass, a toothpick, and paper.
2. Cut the lemon in half.
3. Squeeze the lemon juice into the glass.
4. Soften the toothpick point in the juice.
5. Use the toothpick to write a lemon-juice message on paper.
6. Hold the message above a lamp.
7. Wait for the heat to reveal letters on the paper.
8. Read the secret message.

4. Topic: ______________________

1. Get an empty, clean milk carton; scissors; yarn; and small seeds.
2. Cut a big, round hole on one side of the milk carton.
3. Use the scissors to poke a small hole at the top of the carton.
4. Pull yarn through the small hole.
5. Tie ends of yarn together to make a hanger.
6. Pour the seeds inside the milk carton.
7. Hang the milk carton on a tree branch.
8. Refill with seeds as necessary.

Name ______________________________ Date ______________________________

A Speech to Inform

You give this kind of speech to teach something to an audience. Although you don't have to demonstrate how to do anything, you can if you think a demonstration fits into your speech.

Put stars by the four topics that interest you the most.

recreational vehicles	the Great Barrier Reef	the Pony Express
space exploration	exploring the Arctic	the Winter Olympics
ice cream	luge	Tiger Woods
movie monsters	radar	theme parks
the Pyramids	the microscope	genealogy
plastics	sharks	Hollywood

To inform people, you must give them all the facts. Do this by using the "**5Ws**, plus an **H**," as good reporters do—**Who? What? When? Where? Why?** and **How?**

Read this short speech. Then answer the questions on page 13.

More than 100 years ago, a scientist named Marsh discovered a huge brontosaurus skeleton. Marsh dug it out of the hard and dusty mud, bone by bone. He gathered up other bones he found nearby, wrapped everything, and shipped them to the museum where he worked. Back home he reassembled the skeleton. He topped it with a skull he had found near the skeleton. Soon museums around the world copied Marsh's brontosaurus model. Books and even cartoons, such as *The Flintstones*, made dinosaurs look just like his model.

Over time, some scientists argued that the mouth on Marsh's model wouldn't have allowed the animal to eat properly. One hundred years later, a museum worker found the real brontosaurus' head. It was stored with Marsh's other dinosaur bones. Now everyone had to change the heads on pictures and models to look like the real brontosaurus! That was bad, but the worst was yet to come. A few years later scientists discovered that the brontosaurus wasn't a brontosaurus at all. Its real name was apatosaurus! So museums and books had to change all their information about this dinosaur again. Poor apatosaurus—wrong head, wrong name. What else could go wrong?

Name ______________________ Date ______________________

A Speech to Inform (cont.)

1. Who found the dinosaur bones? ______________________
2. What kind of dinosaur did he think it was? ______________________
3. When did he find the bones? ______________________
4. Where did he send the bones? ______________________
5. Why did scientists think the mouth wasn't right? ______________________
6. How did Marsh make such a mistake? ______________________

It's important to get the audience to see, hear, smell, and feel what you're talking about. Read the following speech excerpts. Underline words or phrases that help you hear, see, smell, feel, or taste what the speaker discussed.

1. Scientists say a volcano is extinct when vents in its crater are blocked by solid lava. But unlike extinct dinosaurs, extinct volcanoes can awaken and blow their tops! That's what happened to Mount St. Helens. In 1980, after 120 years of inactivity, it woke with a loud roar. Then BOOM! It blew its top, sending clouds of smoke into the air. The eruption killed 60 people and spewed volcanic ash over four states. Some places were knee-deep in the cinders!

2. The North American Indians discovered the secret of tapping maple trees. The sweet-water sap flows when a time of freezing is followed by a time of thawing. Last spring I helped my uncle and aunt make syrup. First, we drilled holes into the trees. Next, with a BANG BANG BANG, my uncle hammered a spout into each hole. We attached a bucket to catch the dripping liquid. My aunt and I boiled down the sap into a sticky syrup. The kitchen filled with a sweet maple-y smell. At last, I poured some onto a spoon and tasted it! Mmmm—I couldn't believe I made it!

3. Have you ever been so cold that your teeth chattered? What was the temperature that day? It couldn't have been as low as the -128.6° F recorded in Antarctica! That icy continent holds the world's record for the lowest temperature ever. Here in North America, we think cold is when you can see your breath. But in Antarctica, cold is what keeps the land nearly void of plant and animal life. Creatures are found in the surrounding seas, which are warmer than the land.

Name ______________________ Date ______________________

A Speech to Persuade

You give this kind of speech to get people to change their opinions or to do something. Your topic has two sides, or points of view.

A debate is a special way to give a persuasive speech. Two speakers "face off" against each other in a battle of ideas. One speaks for the idea, and the other speaks against it. Each speaker tries to get the audience to think he or she is right. Usually, as in political debates, each speaker is strongly for or against a topic. But in "mock" debates, a speaker might not agree with the position he or she is asked to defend.

Below are some topics other fifth graders chose for persuasive speeches. Are there really two sides to each topic? Put stars by the four topics that interest you the most.

shorter school days	clean our polluted air	school prayer
school dance every Friday	physical education every day	build homeless shelters
English as the national language	allow students to have cell phones in school	have one no-homework night a week
allow chewing gum	no tests on Fridays	club time during school
replace old desks	new school mascot	health insurance for all
border patrols	movie violence	curfews
school testing	Internet safety	no minimum wage
computer hacking	a woman for President	smoking ads
fat-free lunches	a new recycling plant	solar energy

Name ______________________ Date ______________________

A Speech to Persuade (cont.)

Read Shannon's persuasive speech and answer the questions.

Did you know that the average American throws away about five pounds of trash a day? That's over half a ton a year! Where does it go? For years, we piled it up in landfills, a nice name for dumps. Mountains of trash and garbage were covered with dirt or plastic and then left to rot. Unfortunately, that didn't happen. For decay to occur, there must be enough air and moisture for bacteria to grow. The necessary bacteria didn't grow inside the dumps' covered heaps. How do we know? Garbologists from The University of Arizona dug into an old landfill. What they discovered surprised them. They found 50-year-old newspapers they could still read! The papers helped them date the layer of trash. In the trash they also found an ear of corn (with kernels still on it), green grass clippings, and a hot dog!

Even if we could figure out how to build a landfill that really rots, Earth is running out of space. The best way to solve our trash problem is to make less of it! Recycle. Buy things made from or packaged in recycled material. And complain to companies that overpackage products with extra paper or boxes. Please do your part. Recycle, reuse, and reduce waste. Help save Earth before it's just one big garbage dump!

1. A good title for Shannon's speech would be—
   A. "How to Build a Landfill."
   B. "Solving Our Trash Problem."
   C. "Vote for Shannon Smith."
   D. "Pollution Is Everywhere."

2. Shannon wants the audience to—
   A. recycle materials.
   B. buy items made of recycled materials.
   C. complain to companies that overpackage their products.
   D. all of the above

3. What are three main points Shannon made in her speech?
   A. ______________________
   B. ______________________
   C. ______________________

Name ________________________ Date ________________________

A Speech to Entertain

This is when you want the audience to laugh with you. Many people think this kind of speech is the hardest one to give. But others think it's the easiest. You don't have to convince the audience to do anything or feel a certain way; you just want them to have a good time.

Think about something funny that happened to you or someone you know. When something funny happens, the people involved may not think it's very funny. But later, when they tell others about what happened, they see the humor in it! They probably add details that make the story seem even funnier. Their friends picture it happening and they laugh.

Put stars by the four topics that interest you the most.

the home haircut disaster	a visit to the haunted house	the unraveled sweater
giving medicine to a sick cat	sugar, not salt, in your tea	the faulty vacuum cleaner
wallpapering my room	kitchen problems	losing Aunt Kathy
the runaway wagon	my lost snake	the tub overflows
the stumbling referee	the runaway foul ball	shrinking the laundry
the best knock-knock jokes	spaghetti everywhere	He knows karate?
training a bird	going in the wrong door	the dog ate my book
my dad's birthday gift	learning to pitch	making ice cream
teaching math to my little sister	making balloon animals	the upside-down map

Name ______________________________ Date ______________________________

A Speech to Entertain (cont.)

Antonio gave a speech to entertain his classmates. Read the speech and answer the questions.

Last summer my family took a trip to visit my dad's hometown. Mom and Dad rode up front, and I was squeezed between my two little sisters in the backseat. One had sticky fingers from a lollipop, she was drooling, and she thought I was a towel! Anyway, Mom had this map and she kept trying to get Dad to look at it. "Honey, I don't need a map! I used to live here," he said. Well, suddenly Mom said, "I think we're lost. Why don't you stop at that gas station and ask for directions?" Was she kidding? My dad ask for directions? No way! He took a quick peek at the map and then turned down an old road. We must have been on this road for hours! I was choking on the dust that drifted in the windows! Finally, he stopped. Was he going to ask for directions? Dad looked at Mom. "I think maybe we are lost," he said. He picked up the map and pointed. "We should be right here ...What? Oh, no!" he said and began to laugh. Then he turned the map right-side up. He had been looking at it upside down! "Remember to read a map the right way, kids," he laughed as we drove away. About a mile down the road, Dad asked for directions, and we finally arrived. On the way home, Dad actually used the map right-side up.

1. Antonio gave this speech to—
   A. persuade people to visit their hometown.
   B. teach people about family trips.
   C. entertain people with a funny story.
   D. demonstrate how to read a road map.

2. What was funny about Antonio's sister?
   A. She was squeezed in the backseat.
   B. She wiped her sticky hands on Antonio.
   C. She liked to eat lollipops.
   D. She couldn't read the map.

3. How did Antonio help the audience feel, taste, and see what he did?
   A. by telling that he was squeezed in the back
   B. by telling about choking on the dust
   C. by telling about his dad reading the map upside down
   D. all of the above

4. What do you think was the funniest part of Antonio's speech?

____

Name ______________________ Date ______________________

Research

Your next step is to decide what you're going to say. In order to do this, discover what you know and don't know about your topic. Research your topic using books, magazines, or the Internet. You can also interview people who are knowledgeable about your topic.

A **K-W-L** chart can help you plan your research. The **K** stands for "What I **K**now," the **W** for "What I **W**ant to Know," and the **L** for "What I **L**earned." Below is the beginning of Ruth's chart for research on gorillas. Answer the questions below.

K	W	L
• Gorillas are the largest apes. • Gorillas are endangered. • Gorillas are social animals. • Some gorillas have been taught to use sign language. • Some scientists have lived in the jungle with gorillas. • Gorillas live in the wild in Africa.	• Where in Africa do gorillas live? • How many gorillas are there in the world? • How big do they grow to be? • What do they eat? • How do they interact with each other and with humans? • How do they learn sign language? • Why are they endangered? • Can zoos help to save gorillas?	• Different species live in the lowlands and mountains of Africa. • There are thousands of lowland gorillas, but only 650 mountain gorillas are left in the world.

1. Where could Ruth find the most information about gorilla habitats?

____

2. How could she find out whether zoos can help save gorillas?

____

3. Where could she learn more about gorillas and sign language?

____

Name ______________________________ Date ______________________________

Making Notes and Cue Cards

Take notes on 3" x 5" cards as you research your topic. Write only key words or phrases, not whole sentences. Write just one fact on each card.

Arrange the cards to form a fact web, with your topic as the middle card. Does your web make sense? Can you see how the facts might work together in a speech? Make sure you don't include too many or too few facts for the length of your speech. Add or remove cards from the web until you're satisfied.

Look at Eric's fact web about snails.

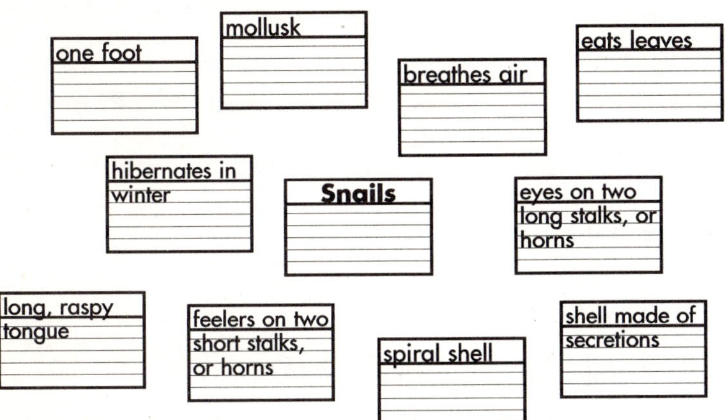

Create a web of notes from the paragraph below. Add more circles if necessary.

The first modern-day computer in the United States was ENIAC. Built at the University of Pennsylvania in 1945, ENIAC weighed about 30 tons. It had thousands of electrical switches, called vacuum tubes, which allowed the computer to do mathematical calculations. ENIAC was useful, but it had no "memory" for storing data. Soon scientists developed computers with memory. The first ones still filled entire rooms. They weren't very fast, but they could be programmed to work through the night while workers slept. Everything changed in 1947, when the transistor was invented. It weighed a hundred times less than a vacuum tube, broke down far less frequently, and was much faster. Then in 1971, the microchip was created. It could run an entire computer. One microchip about the size of a penny can hold more than 200,000 transistors!

Name ______________________ Date ______________________

Outlining

Now you are ready to use your research notes to make an outline.

An outline has three parts:

Main Topics: labeled with Roman numerals I, II, and so on; first word capitalized

Subtopics: indented to show relationship to the main topic; labeled A, B, and so on; first word capitalized

Details: indented to show relation to the subtopic; labeled 1, 2, and so on; first word capitalized

Helpful Hint: In an outline, if there's a I, there must be a II; if there's an A, there must be a B; and if there's a 1, there must be a 2.

Look at Charlie's outline below. Answer the questions about the outline.

Animal Protection

I. Animal coverings
   A. Fur
   B. Feathers
   C. Shells
   D. Scales
II. Special features
   A. Coloration
      1. Hiding in plain sight
      2. Attracting a mate
   B. Skunk's odor
   C. Porcupine's quills
      1. Myths about "shooting"
      2. Truth about "releasing"
   D. Claws
      1. For climbing and digging
      2. For fighting
III. Animal senses

1. What's the title of the speech?

____

2. What are the three main topics?

____

____

____

3. What are the four subtopics under topic I?

____

____

____

____

4. What are the two details under subtopic C for topic II?

____

____

Name ______________________________ Date ______________________________

Outlining (cont.)

Read Lorainne's speech about George Washington. Help her fill in the missing parts of her outline below.

George Washington was born in 1732 in Virginia. When he was 11, his father died. George was taught at home before going to the Henry William's school. He was good in math and mapmaking. At 16, he was hired to survey land beyond the Blue Ridge Mountains. This hard work took more than a year. In 1749, he was appointed to his first public office, surveyor of Culpepper County. As a lieutenant colonel in the French and Indian War, he escaped injury, although two of his horses were shot. He married his wife, Martha, in 1759 and settled at Mount Vernon. In May of 1775, he was elected Commander of the Army. On July 3, he led his troops into a war that lasted until 1781. He played an important part in the Constitutional Convention of 1787. After the Constitution was adopted, he was unanimously chosen to be the first U.S. President. On April 30, 1789, he took the oath of office. He retired at the end of his second term and returned to Mount Vernon.

Title: ______________________________

I. Childhood
  A. ______________________________
  B. His father dies
  C. Is a student
    1. Good in math
    2. ______________________________
II. Surveyor
  A. Surveyed land beyond ______________________________
  B. Appointed surveyor at age 17
III. Military career
  A. French and Indian War
    1. ______________________________
    2. Had two of his horses shot
  B. Revolutionary War
    1. Commander
    2. ______________________________
IV. Married Martha
V. Presidency
  A. ______________________________
  B. ______________________________

Name ______________________ Date ______________________

Grammar Check

You're almost ready to start writing.

But first, you must review some language rules.

- A **sentence** tells a complete idea.
- All sentences begin with a **capital letter**.
- Different kinds of sentences have different end marks.

Example	Sentence Kind	End Mark
Today is Friday.	statement	period (.)
Where is your hat?	question	question (?)
Don't eat too much.	command	period (.)
Turn left now!	command (urgent)	exclamation (!)
The volcano is erupting!	exclamation	exclamation (!)

- Every sentence has two parts: the **subject** and the **predicate**.
- A **noun** names a person, place, or thing.
- A **verb** tells a state of being or what is happening, has happened, or will happen.
- A **pronoun** takes the place of a noun.
- An **adjective** describes a noun.
- An **adverb** tells more about a verb.
- A **simile** uses *like* or *as* to compare two things.
- A **metaphor** compares two things without using *like* or *as*.

Read each group of words below. If it's a sentence, supply the proper end mark. If it's not a sentence, finish it and add an end mark.

1. I know this belongs ______________________
2. Why didn't you call me last week ______________________
3. That is the most phenomenal outfit ______________________
4. The bird swooped down to ______________________
5. Don't ever do that again ______________________
6. Where is the ______________________
7. Please just sit down and ______________________
8. I forgot to do my homework and ______________________

Name ______________________ Date ______________________

Grammar Check (cont.)

Rewrite each group of words so the sentences makes sense.

1. that's don't funny think I!

____

2. do your to remember Please homework.

____

3. remember of can't I song that name the.

____

4. completed assigned by your Have date project the.

____

Draw a line to match each subject with its predicate.

Subject	**Predicate**
5. That movie	A. tastes like Italy itself.
6. My mom's spaghetti	B. gives too much homework!
7. Our old dog	C. have always been best friends.
8. The new teacher	D. was a remake of one I used to love!
9. You and I	E. chases its tail all day!

Circle the correct word in each sentence.

10. (We, Us) always go to the parade with (him, his) father.
11. Please give those books to (her, she) and (I, me).
12. (Them, They) never let us borrow (their, they) CDs.
13. Joanna can't find (her, she) homework because someone (hided, hid) it.
14. (He, Him) told us it was okay if Justin (come, came) along to the party.
15. Read the following simile: *Her dress was as green as the grass.* Now write a simile using one of these topics: *clouds, eyes, hair,* or *sandwich.*

____

____

16. Read the following metaphor: *I have a mountain of work to do.* Now write a metaphor using the following phrase: *monster of a storm.*

____

____

Name ________________________________ Date ________________________________

The Speech: The Opening

Since your audience will *hear* what you have to say instead of *read* what you have to say, you need to use as many short, simple sentences as you can. You must make everything clear the first time you say it. Your audience can't rewind you and play your speech again!

The opening of your speech is very important. It helps you grab the audience's attention. Experts say the best speech openings are short, just two to four sentences long. Begin your speech with the main idea. This should make your audience want to listen.

Here are a few popular ways to begin a speech. Notice that each opening is just a few sentences. Write your own speech openings below.

- **Start with a quote:** Coach Vince Lombardi said, "Some people try to find things in this game that don't exist, but football is only two things—blocking and tackling." Well, let's look at some of the greatest blockers and tacklers the sport has known.
- **Start with an interesting fact:** A duck's quack doesn't echo—and no one knows why. Today we'll investigate how echoes are produced and how other animals use them to find food.
- **Start with humor:** We know that foamy popcorn is used in shipping and packing. But have you ever touched it and wondered what it is? Or have you ever wondered what people ship the popcorn in? Let's take a closer look at the properties of packing popcorn.
- **Start with a simple fact:** The average person laughs about 15 times a day. But doctors say we should laugh more often. Let's find out why.
- **Start with a question:** Can animals really talk to people?

1. Start by telling something about yourself.

____

____

2. Start with an interesting fact.

____

____

3. Start with a simple question.

____

____

Name ______________________ Date ______________________

The Speech: The Opening (cont.)

Helpful Hints

Remember, the opening for a speech:

- must grab people's attention.
- has a topic sentence that tells the main idea.
- should be short, just a few lines.

Write an opening for a speech on each of the topics below. Use humor, a quote, or any other way explained on page 24. Make each opening just a few sentences—the shorter, the better. When you're finished, keep this paper. You'll need it later when you learn about writing the middle part of a speech.

1. basketball ______________________

2. music television ______________________

3. the Olympic Games ______________________

4. the Internet ______________________

5. weather ______________________

Name ______________________ Date ______________________

The Speech: The Body

The middle, or body, of your speech should be the longest part. It will include a paragraph to cover each of the main topics in your outline. Look at the topics, subtopics, and details you listed in your outline. Use the outline and your notes to organize your ideas into a speech. Make sure you put the facts in a logical order. And try to use as many short, simple sentences as possible.

Read Marcus's speech about George Washington Carver.

George Washington Carver was born in Missouri in 1864. As a child, he became interested in plants. People called him "the plant doctor." When he was 12, he went away to school. He got a job to pay his way and lived with families who would take him in. By 1896, he had earned two college degrees. He became a teacher and researcher at the Tuskegee Institute in Alabama.

Carver is best known for his work in agriculture. As head of research, he worked to develop new ideas that would help poor Southern farmers. Most of them grew only cotton on their farms. But year after year, the crops suffered. Carver knew the cotton was taking the nitrogen out of the soil. So he suggested that farmers alternate a year of growing cotton and a year of growing peanuts, soybeans, or sweet potatoes since those plants put nitrogen into the soil as they grow. When Southern farmers began to rotate those crops with cotton, they earned more money.

Carver experimented to develop new products made from peanuts and sweet potatoes. From peanuts, he made more than 300 products, including coffee, cheese, milk, ink, flour, and soap! He also made more than 100 products from sweet potatoes, including molasses, flour, rubber, and glue! George Washington Carver received many honors, but he was most proud of the work he had done to help the farmers.

What are the three main topics in Marcus's speech?

____

____

____

Name ______________________ Date ______________________

The Speech: The Body (cont.)

Look back at the openings you wrote on page 25. Choose a topic from that page that you already know enough about so you don't have to research it. Write the body of your speech below.

Now choose a new topic and write any kind of speech you want. You might write a speech about healthy snacks to **inform** people why some foods are more healthful than others. Or you might write a speech to **persuade** people to eat more healthful snacks. Share your speech with your classmates. Then keep it to use when you learn about writing the end of a speech.

Helpful Hint:

Keep it simple. A speech should not be too long **or** too short.

Name ______________________________ Date ______________________________

The Speech: The Conclusion

A good speechmaker ends a speech by summarizing the main idea of the speech. About speeches, some speech experts say, "First tell people what you're going to tell them (the opening), then tell it to them (the body), and finally tell them what you told them (the conclusion)."

The easiest way to summarize a speech is to refer directly back to the introduction. Try to use the same technique for the conclusion that you used for the opening—humor or a fact. Using the same technique helps keep your speech consistent. And like the opening, the conclusion should only be a few lines.

Below are five conclusions to five different speeches. See if you can determine the topic of each speech.

1. The next time I try to build a model airplane, I'll use the instructions that come with it so I get it right the first time. Topic: ______________________________
2. The weather was perfect. The views were breathtaking. And the people were so friendly. I would go back to Hawaii in a heartbeat. Topic: ______________________________
3. Our kids need our help in restoring their playground back to its original state. I hope to see you all here this Saturday. Without your help, the playground won't last much longer. Topic: ______________________________
4. As you can see, the giraffe is one of the most unique animals in the world. What other animal can eat from the treetops without having to stand on its tippy-toes? Topic: ______________
5. And finally, when you're ready to serve your hot cheddar dip, make sure you surround it with crispy bread rounds. After all of the time and hard work you spent preparing it, you want your friends to be able to dip in! Topic: ______________________________

Name ______________________________ Date ______________________________

The Speech: The Conclusion (cont.)

Helpful Hints

Remember, the conclusion of a speech should:

- summarize the main idea.
- let the audience know the speech is over.
- be short, just a few lines.

Reread the opening you chose from page 25 for the body of the speech on page 27. Also reread the body of your speech on page 27. Now your speech is ready for a conclusion.

Look back at your topic sentence. It announced what you were going to tell the audience. Find a way to end your speech by reminding your audience of your main idea. Use a question, humor, a number, or another technique you think will work. If you chose to write a persuasive speech, be sure to end by asking your audience to take action.

Keep your conclusion short. When you've finished writing your conclusion below, share it with the class.

____

____

____

____

____

____

____

____

____

____

____

____

____

____

Helpful Hint:

Leave a lasting impression. Remember to end with a smile.

Name ______________________________ Date ______________________________

Read and Revise

Read your speech to yourself. Do you like the way it sounds? Is it arranged in a logical order? If it's too long or too short, now is the time to make changes.

Also, look carefully at your speech for spelling and grammatical errors. You may wonder why that matters since people will hear your words, and not see them. But someone may ask for a copy of your speech if they really liked it. Use the checklist below as you look over your speech.

Speech Checklist

_____ Does my speech include everything from my outline?
_____ Is my speech well organized?
_____ Should I add/remove anything?
_____ Could I improve on the opening?
_____ Are there enough interesting facts to keep people listening?
_____ Could I improve the conclusion?
_____ Are there any grammatical/spelling errors?

Look at the speech below, and correct the spelling and grammatical errors. Then rewrite it correctly on another sheet of paper.

The Pilgrms

The Pilgrims sailed frm Plymouth, England, on the *Mayflower* on Septemer 6, 1620. There wes 102 pazzengers on bored. the beginning of the voyage were pleaseant. But many pasengers were seesick. Then the ship runned into storms and high winds. Beams on deck cracking and let water leak into the ship. A sailor and a Pilgrim died on the vouyage, and one baby was born. He saw named "Oceanus." On Novmber 9, 1620, people on the *Mayflower* sited land. It was where is now Cape Cod. Two days later, after 66 days at sea, the ship droped it's ancor. Some of the Pilgrims going ashore. they bilt a village at what is today Plymouth, Masacusetts They seen some Native Americans from afar, but didn't meet them intil March of the next year. Massasoit, an Indian leader, suggested the Pilgrims plant crops of weat, barley, Indin corn, and peas. At harvest time, the Pilgrims invited Massasoit and his people to celebrat with them. Now we remeber there celebration on our Thankgiving Day.

Name ______________________________ Date ______________________________

Choosing and Using Visual Aids

People who make speeches often use visual aids, such as pictures, posters, graphs, real objects, or a demonstrated action. The visual aids show the audience how something looks, stress important information, or just add interest to a speech.

If you plan to use a visual aid, here are a few things to consider.

Will it be seen? Imagine that you're sitting at the back of the room during your speech. Would you be able to see the details on your poster board or in your picture? If not, the visual aid won't help your presentation. Forget it and try something else.

Will it help or be a distraction? Will the visual aid you plan to use take people's attention away from what you're saying? Does it encourage people to start conversations *with each other* during your speech? If so, the visual aid is a distraction, not a help. Don't use it!

Helpful Hints

When picking a visual aid, remember:

- to make sure it refers to just one idea.
- to use simple words.
- to make graphs colorful and easy to understand.
- to check your spelling.

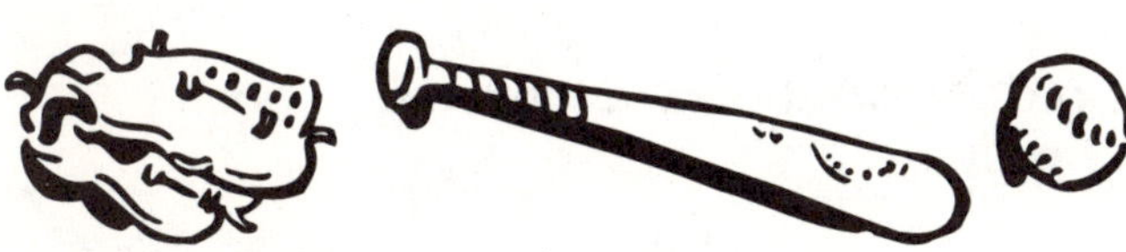

Imagine you're planning a speech about your favorite sport. List the visual aids you would use during your speech and how you would use them.

Sports Visual Aids

____

____

____

____

Name ______________________ Date ______________________

Delivery: Your Voice

What you say in your speech is important. But how you say it is just as important. When people listen to you, they should be able to hear and understand you. Use your voice as a tool. Learn to **project**, or throw, your voice so everyone can hear you clearly. You want every person to think you're speaking just to him or her. You can also use your voice to let people know which points in your speech are most important. To do that, emphasize particular words or facts.

Helpful Hints

- Pronounce your words clearly and carefully.
- Use words that everyone can understand.
- Speak slowly enough so people can understand you.
- Vary the speed of your voice so you don't sound bored.
- Vary the pitch and volume of your voice to stress words.
- Pause to stress a point or to give the audience time to react.
- Talk to the audience the same way you'd talk to a friend.
- Be yourself. Don't try to imitate other speakers you've heard.

Read each sentence aloud. Stress the underlined word. Notice how the meaning of each sentence changes.

<u>This</u> is not funny!
This <u>is</u> not funny!
This is <u>not</u> funny!
This is not <u>funny</u>!

On the lines below, write one sentence three times. For each sentence, stress a different word. Underline the word you stressed. Notice how the meaning of the sentence changes.

____

____

____

Name ______________________ Date ______________________

Delivery: Your Body Language

People from different countries speak different languages. We may not always understand what they say, but people everywhere speak the same body language. So how you look during your speech is as important as what you say and how you sound.

Helpful Hints

- Stand up straight. Keep your feet slightly apart.
- Balance your weight on both feet. Don't sway back and forth.
- Keep your hands out of your pockets and off your hips.
- Look from person to person to make eye contact with everyone.
- Smile, unless you're saying something sad or serious.
- Use your hands for meaningful gestures.
- Try not to fidget.
- Let your personality show through. Don't be afraid to show feelings.

Oddly enough, most communication is nonverbal. For example, a friend is listening to a CD. You ask if he wants a snack. He shakes his head side to side for "no" and up and down for "yes." You ask, "Where's my book?" He points instead of saying, "Over there."

Act out these body-language skits with classmates. Then create two more skits for the class to do.

1. You and two friends are together. Your two friends are talking to each other and not including you in the conversation. How do you react—without using words?
2. You just burned your tongue on a piece of pizza. Now your friend is about to bite into a piece. How do you warn him or her?

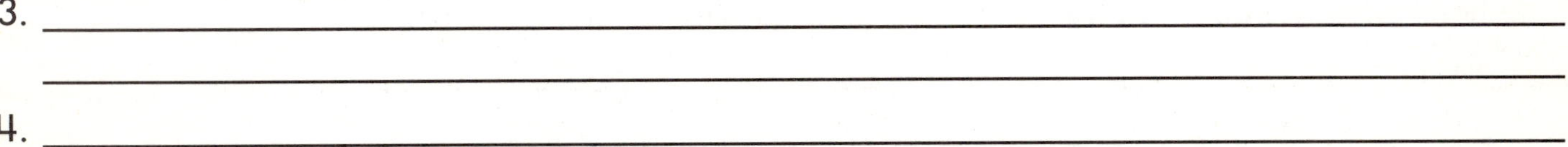

3. ____

4. ____

Name ______________________________ Date ______________________________

Practice and Check

You've written your speech, chosen your visual aids, and made your cue cards. Now it's time to practice.

Practice in front of a mirror or for a friend as if it were the real deal. If you have a tape recorder or a video camera, record your speech and review it later. Use a checklist like the one below after you're done.

Speech Checklist

_____ Did I dress neatly and comfortably?

_____ Did I stand straight and tall?

_____ Did I smile?

_____ Did I speak clearly?

_____ Did I project my voice correctly?

_____ Did I change my pitch and volume?

_____ Did I use gestures properly?

_____ Did I use my visual aids effectively?

_____ Did I look at my notes too often?

_____ Did I get—and keep—the audience's attention?

_____ Did I make eye contact with everyone?

_____ Did I cover all of my facts and ideas?

_____ Did I accomplish my goal to demonstrate, inform, persuade, or entertain?

_____ Did I stay within the time limit?

What other questions might you add to the checklist?

____

Answer the questions below.

1. What are three areas you need to work on before giving your speech?

____

____

2. What should you do if you answered "no" to a question on the checklist?

____

____

Helpful Hint:

Memorize only the first and last lines of your speech. That way you can maintain eye contact with your audience as you begin and end your speech.

Name ______________________________ Date ______________________________

Nerves: Good News or Bad?

Do you get nervous before speaking in front of people? Don't worry about it. Even famous actors admit to being nervous before performing. They want to do their best, so they worry.

Here are a few things you can do to help you relax before giving a speech.

- Make sure you've prepared and practiced your speech.
- Wear something comfortable.
- Do some exercises, such as walking or jogging.
- Do deep breathing exercises. Inhale through your nose. Hold your breath and count to five. Then breathe out to the count of ten.
- Shake out your body like you're a rag doll.
- Open and close your fists.
- Pace back and forth if it helps you get rid of nervous energy.
- Visualize the audience enjoying your speech—because they will!

During your speech:

- use your 3" x 5" cue cards to keep you on track.
- make eye contact with a friendly face in the audience.
- pause and take a deep breath.
- remember why you chose the topic—because it interested you! Make sure it shows.

Think of three more tips that will help you perform at your best.

1. ______________________________
2. ______________________________
3. ______________________________

Name ______________________ Date ______________________

Examine a Speech

Alicia wrote a short speech about honeybees.

Read her speech and answer the questions.

Did you know that honeybees dance? It's true! They dance to tell other bees where to find nectar. Let's say this bee finds juicy nectar in one of these flowers. The bee fills its honey sac with some nectar and then buzzes back to the beehive. Inside the hive, the bee begins to dance. The other bees stop what they're doing to watch. The dancing bee spells out the direction of the nectar-filled flowers. If the flowers are not too far from the hive, the bee dances circles on the honeycomb, going in one direction, then the other. If the flowers are farther away, the bee does a "waggle" dance. It ceaselessly moves across the honeycomb in a figure-eight pattern. If the nectar is toward the sun, the little bee moves up the honeycomb. If the nectar is away from the sun, the bee moves down the honeycomb. The bee moves to the right if the nectar is to the right of the sun and to the left if the nectar is to the left of the sun. The closer the nectar is to the beehive, the faster the little bee dances. All the other bees can smell the nectar on the dancing bee. They start to copy its movements to let the bee know they understand. Then they all leave the hive. The bees fly in bigger and bigger circles until they discover where the nectar-filled flowers are. Then it's feast time for everyone!

So you see, you don't always have to SAY what you mean. You could communicate through dance, like the honeybees!

1. What is the topic of the speech?
   A. the history of dance
   B. famous ballet stars
   C. the bee dance
   D. taming bees

2. What kind of speech is it?
   A. a speech to inform
   B. a speech to demonstrate
   C. a speech to persuade
   D. none of the above

3. Alicia opens her speech by—
   A. using a quote.
   B. asking a question.
   C. linking it to another speech.
   D. using humor.

Name ______________________________ Date ______________________________

Examine a Speech (cont.)

4. What does Alicia want you to know about communicating?
   A. There are different ways to communicate ideas.
   B. A dance can communicate an idea.
   C. Insects communicate with one another.
   D. all of the above
5. What visual aids could Alicia have used? Where during the speech could she have used them?

____

____

6. Which words or phrases do you think Alicia stressed? Underline them in the speech.

Now plan a short speech about a topic of your choice. Fill in the outline below. Use the outline to help you write your speech. Remember to read your speech aloud several times. Give the speech to your classmates when you're ready.

1. What kind of speech will it be?

____

2. What will the topic be?

____

3. How will your opening grab everyone's attention?

____

____

4. What do you want people to know about the topic?

____

____

____

5. How will you end the speech?

____

____

6. What visuals, if any, will you use?

____

Write your speech on a separate sheet of paper.

Name ______________________ Date ______________________

Interview and Introduce

A good way to get over the fear of public speaking is to talk about someone else.

Choose a subject—the person can be real or fictional. The goal of the assignment is to tell as many interesting facts about the person as you can without using his or her name. Interview the person (if real), and fill in the chart below. Add some questions of your own. Then write a short speech about the person. Don't tell the person's name until the end. Show a picture of the person if possible.

Interesting Facts	Notes
When and where was this person born?	
Is he or she from a large or small family?	
Where did he or she go to school?	
What does he or she do for fun?	
What's the best thing to happen to him or her?	
What's the worst thing to happen to him or her?	
Why do you like him or her?	
How do you know this person?	

Name ______________________________ Date ______________________________

Interview and Introduce (cont.)

Read the speech below that Elizabeth wrote about her favorite fictional character.

The person I'd like to introduce may not be real, but she likes the same thing I do—horses. She grew up in England, where she lived with her parents, a younger brother, and an older sister. She was a happy girl, even when she had to wear braces on her teeth. But she was happiest when she was around horses. Luckily for her, a beautiful horse came to live with her family when she was about 12 years old. She loved to care for him and ride him—especially when he ran flat out and she could feel the wind whipping through her hair!

A boy came to stay with the family and take care of the horse. He knew the fast horse could be a racehorse. Not everyone agreed. But this girl knew the animal had a great heart. So she helped train the horse for the biggest race in England. On the day of the race, there wasn't a jockey to ride the great horse. This brave girl cut off her hair so she looked more like a boy! Then she climbed into the saddle and rode the horse in the race. After the race, people were shocked to discover that a girl, not a boy, had won the race! She's my hero because I wish I could ride in a race too. I'm happy to present Velvet Brown, heroine of the book *National Velvet*.

Think about the following as you write your speech.

How can you grab the audience's attention without using the person's name?

____

____

What facts about the person do you want to include in your speech?

____

____

How will you end your speech?

____

____

Helpful Hint:

Use a pause to stress something important in your speech. As you practice your speech, write *(Pause)* to show where you want to pause during the speech.

Name ______________________ Date ______________________

Accept an Award

Are you a good athlete? Do you like to sing? Do you look forward to auditioning for the school play? Are you a genius at math or science? Everyone has something he or she does well. And most people dream about someday being rewarded for their talent. Maybe you'll be voted MVP of a World Series; win an Oscar, an Emmy, a Tony, or a Grammy, or win the Pulitzer Prize in literature or the Nobel Prize in mathematics. If you've ever pretended to give an acceptance speech, you're not alone. Millions of people do the same thing. They know exactly what they'll say if the big day ever arrives.

What kind of award would you like to receive? What would you say if it were given to you? Use the outline below to plan a short acceptance speech. Underline words you want to emphasize. Make any visual aids you'd like to use. Then practice the speech and present it to your class. Ask a classmate to introduce you and give you the imaginary award.

1. What award would you want to win?

____

2. Who would be in your audience?

____

____

3. What are the main points you would cover in your speech?

____

____

____

4. Who would you take to the awards ceremony with you? Why?

____

____

5. What visual aids, if any, would you use?

____

Name ______________________________ Date ______________________________

Make a Public Announcement

People make announcements over school PA systems so everyone can hear what's going on at the same time. Announcements may be about the weather, class photos, trips, or other school events.

Your principal wants you to write an announcement about the school event below.

Your school is planning a fund-raising carnival on Saturday, March 12, from 9 A.M. to 7:30 P.M. All the money raised will go toward buying new computers for the school. Each grade is responsible for a booth or game at the carnival. One class has face painting; another, spin art; another, bowling; and another, balloon animals. Your fifth-grade class is running a ring-toss game. People will have a chance to win prizes. There will be food to eat and a bake sale. A DJ from a local radio show will spin records for dancing in the school gym from 4 P.M. until 7 P.M. The games will be played outdoors, unless it rains. If it rains, everything will move inside to the classrooms. Tickets for the top prize at the carnival, a big-screen TV donated by a local store, are $1 each or six tickets for $5.

What do you want to include in your two-minute announcement?

1. What kind of event is it?

____

2. When is it? (day, date, time)

____

3. What kinds of things can people do?

____

4. Who's running the games and booths?

____

5. What can people win? How much are the tickets?

____

6. Who will provide music and where will people dance?

____

7. What will happen if it rains?

____

Use the information above to write a short announcement. Then practice and give your speech to your classmates.

Name ______________________________ Date ______________________________

Give a Review

Critics give informative speeches when they review a new movie. Their reviews are persuasive when they convince you either to see or not to see the film. The reviews may also be entertaining if they include funny things that happened in the movie. Books, CDs, plays, TV shows, and sporting events can also be reviewed.

Fill in the two review forms below about your favorite book and movie. Then choose one and write a review based on your notes.

Book Report

Title of Book

____

Author

____

Illustrator/Photographer

____

Main Topic of the Book

____

List three facts you learned from the book.

1. ______________________________
2. ______________________________
3. ______________________________

Give reasons why you think others will like the book.

____

____

Movie Review

Title of Movie

____

Stars of Movie

____

Kind of Movie (mystery, comedy, cartoon, adventure, drama)

____

List two reasons why you liked the movie.

1. ______________________________
2. ______________________________

Give reasons why you think others will like the movie.

____

____

Name ______________________ Date ______________________

Be Entertaining

Write and give an entertaining speech. Use a topic from page 16, use one of the scenarios below, or come up with your own idea. You might tell about something that really happened to you or someone you know. Your only goal is to make your audience laugh! Your speech should be five minutes long.

- You take your little brother and sister through a haunted house at Halloween. They are afraid of everything from the minute you walk through the door. The two of them scream, jump up and down, and pull on your arms to try to drag you out of the house.
- You can't find your right shoe, and you're late for school. You've already missed the bus. Now your dad is in the car, honking the horn impatiently. You look everywhere for that shoe—except under the dog. He's sleeping on top of it!
- Your sister is crazy about the new boy who moved in next door. She's never met him, but she watches him from afar. Finally, one day she gets up the nerve to go over and talk to him. She's nervous, but doing okay. Then she trips on his front porch and lands at his feet!

Organize your thoughts below. Then write and give your entertaining speech.

1. What will be the topic of your entertaining speech?

____

2. What main ideas will you cover in your speech?

   A. ____

   B. ____

   C. ____

3. What visual aids, if any, will you use?

____

____

Name ______________________ Date ______________________

Be Persuasive

Commercials are short speeches that are meant to be persuasive. They include words and phrases that persuade you to feel a certain way, such as "new and improved" and "the best around." Companies rely on persuasive commercials to sell their products.

You are going to write and give a two-minute persuasive commercial to your class. Choose a product you think you could sell. Organize your thoughts below before writing your speech. Also draw your product in the box below.

1. What is my product?

____

2. What are the main selling points I want to stress in my speech?

____

____

3. How will I make this product appealing to my audience?

____

4. What visual aids, if any, will I use?

____

Write your commercial on a separate sheet of paper, and give it as a speech.

Name ______________________________ Date ______________________________

Speak to a New Audience

Now it's time to move on and use your speech-making skills on other audiences. Marcus gave his speech about George Washington Carver to a fourth-grade class during Black History Month. For visuals, he had a large picture of Carver, a peanut, a sweet potato, and a chart listing all the things Carver made from those foods. Alicia gave her dancing-bee speech to several first-grade classes. They were learning about animal homes, so one of Alicia's visuals was a large drawing of the inside of a hive with the honeycomb. Another visual she used was a stuffed toy bee. Lastly, Alicia wore a headband equipped with pipe-cleaner antennae and demonstrated the dances for the children!

Plan a speech for another group in your school. You might choose to speak to children younger than you. Or you might choose to speak to a parents' or teachers' group. Just check with other teachers or the principal for permission to give your presentation.

1. What topic could you choose that would interest younger students? ______________________

   What topic would interest adults? ______________________________

2. What main ideas would you cover?

   A. ______________________________

   B. ______________________________

   C. ______________________________

3. What visual aids would you use?

   ____

   ____

4. How would you make your speech appropriate for your specific audience?

   ____

   ____

Answer Key

page 5: I. I, 2. P, 3. P, 4. I

page 6: I. D, 2. B, 3. C, 4. F, 5. F

page 7: I. C, 2. A, 3. C

page 8: Topics—Sybil Luddington, Storms, Computers; Main-Idea Statements—Answers will vary but might include these: I. Basketball is a game in which players try to get a ball through a hoop to score points; 2. Magnets are attracted to iron, so they can pick up certain metal objects; 3. Dinosaurs ruled the land millions of years ago but for some reason became extinct; 4. Although it's called music, rap is actually the reading of poetry to a musical background; 5. Pets require care but can be helpful in reducing the stress in people's lives.

page 9: Answers will vary.

page 10: 6, 12, 1, 9, 2, 10, 3, 8, 4, 11, 5, 7

page 11: Wording of answers will vary but should relate to these: Setting the Table; Making Invisible Ink or Writing a Secret Message; Making a Bird Feeder.

page 13: I. Marsh; 2. brontosaurus; 3. over 100 years ago; 4. back to the museum where he worked; 5. it wouldn't have let the brontosaurus eat properly; 6. he picked up a skull that was nearby the skeleton. Sensory Words—Answers will vary but might include these: I. roar, BOOM, clouds of smoke, spewed, knee-deep; 2. sweet-water sap, flows, drilled, BANG, hammered, dripping, boiled, sticky, sweet maple-y smell, tasted, Mmmm; 3. teeth chattered, icy, see your breath, warmer.

page 15: I. B, 2. D, 3. Answers will vary but might include these: The average American throws away about five pounds of trash a day. Trash in landfills doesn't rot because there's not enough air and moisture for bacteria to grow. Garbologists dug into an old landfill and found 50-year-old newspapers they could still read and recognizable food. Earth is running out of space to put landfills. We can make less trash by recycling and reusing materials.

page 17: I. C, 2. B, 3. D, 4. Answers will vary.

page 18: I. In books or on the Internet; 2. Call or write to a local zoo or visit the zoo to talk to zookeepers; 3. Answers will vary but might include an encyclopedia, the NASA Web site, a book about space, older people who watched the moon landing, magazine articles, or a TV show about space.

page 19: The word Computers should be in the center circle. The other words or phrases will vary but might include: ENIAC, first in 1945, weighed 30 tons, had no memory, vacuum tubes, filled a room, transistors in 1947, weighed 100 times less, microchip in 1971, holds more date than 200,000 transistors.

page 20: I. Animal Protection; 2. Animal coverings, Special features, Animal senses; 3. Fur, Feathers, Shells, Scales; 4. Myths about "shooting," Truth about "releasing."

page 21: Title: George Washington; I. A. Born in 1732; C. 2. Good in mapmaking; II. A. Blue Ridge Mountains; III. A. I. Lieutenant colonel; B. 2. Led troops into six-year war; V. A. Elected unanimously; B. Took oath of office April 30, 1789.

page 22: I. Answers will vary, but it should end with a period; 2. question mark; 3. exclamation mark; 4. Answers will vary, but it should end with a period; 5. exclamation mark; 6. Answers will vary, but it should end with a question mark; 7. Answers will vary, but it could end in a period or an exclamation mark; 8. Answers will vary, but it should end with a period.

Answer Key

page 23: 1. I don't think that's funny!; 2. Please remember to do your homework.; 3. I can't remember the name of that song.; 4. Have your project completed by the assigned date. 5. D, 6. A, 7. E, 8. B, 9. C. 10. We/his; 11. her/me; 12. They/their; 13. her/hid; 14. He/came; 15. Answers will vary; 16. Answers will vary.

page 24: Answers will vary.

page 25: Answers will vary.

page 26: Answers will vary.

page 27: Answers will vary.

page 28: Answers will vary.

page 29: Answers will vary.

page 30: The Pilgrims. The Pilgrims sailed from Plymouth, England, on the *Mayflower* on September 6, 1620. There were 102 passengers on board. The beginning of the voyage was pleasant. But many passengers were seasick. Then the ship ran into storms and high winds. Beams on deck cracked and let water leak into the ship. A sailor and a Pilgrim died on the voyage, and one baby was born. He was named "Oceanus." On November 9, 1620, people on the *Mayflower* sighted land. It was where Cape Cod is now. Two days later, after 66 days at sea, the ship dropped its anchor. Some of the Pilgrims went ashore. They built a village at what is today Plymouth, Massachusetts. They saw some Native Americans from afar, but didn't meet them until March of the next year. Massasoit, an Indian leader, suggested the Pilgrims plant crops of wheat, barley, Indian corn, and peas. At harvest time, the Pilgrims invited Massasoit and his people to celebrate with them. Now we remember their celebration on our Thanksgiving Day.

page 31: Answers will vary.

page 32: Answers will vary.

page 33: Answers will vary.

page 34: Answers will vary; 1. Answers will vary; 2. Answers will vary but might include these: practice some more, change parts of the speech, ask a friend or a teacher for advice, concentrate on the problems and how to fix them.

page 35: Answers will vary.

page 36: 1. C, 2. A, 3. B

page 37: 4. D, 5. a picture of a honeybee, a picture of a flower, real flowers, a picture of a honeycomb; to demonstrate how the bee moved and to draw the bee's movements in the hive—circular and figure-eight patterns; 6. Answers will vary but might include these: true, other bees, nectar, this bee, these flowers, honey sac, buzzes, what, direction, from the hive, circles, farther away, waggle, toward, away from, faster, feast time, SAY.

page 38: Answers will vary.

page 39: Answers will vary.

page 40: Answers will vary.

page 41: 1. a carnival; 2. Saturday, March 12, from 9 A.M. to 7:30 P.M.; 3. Answers will vary but might include these: eat, play games, dance, win prizes, buy baked goods; 4. each grade is running a game or booth; 5. a big-screen TV; $1 a ticket or six tickets for $5; 6. a local DJ; in the gym; 7. games will be held in classrooms.

page 42: Answers will vary.

page 43: Answers will vary.

page 44: Answers will vary.

page 45: Answers will vary.

Making Speeches Scoring Rubric

Use this 5-point rubric to score student performance:
4 = Excellent
3 = Good
2 = Average
1 = Poor
0 = Incomplete or unscorable

Student's Name: ______________________________ **Date:** __________

Basic Speech Type: (circle one)
Demonstrative **Informative**

Persuasive **Entertaining**

Name of Speech: ____

SCORE	CRITERIA	ADDITIONAL COMMENTS
	Topic selection: is appropriate for the audience	
	Topic selection: fits the speech type	
	Writing: uses proper sentence structure	
	Writing: uses correct grammar and appropriate language	
	Introduction: gets audience's attention and states purpose	
	Body: is clearly organized and developed	
	Conclusion: wraps up thoughts	
	Delivery: is natural and indicates self-confidence	
	Delivery: uses appropriate posture, eye contact, gestures, and facial expressions	
	Delivery: uses clear articulation and pronunciation, volume, pitch, and pace	
	Visuals: are appropriate and enhance the presentation	
TOTAL		